Colors

Yellow

Nancy Harris

Heinemann Library
Chicago, Illinois

HEINEMANN-RAINTREE

TO ORDER:
☎ Call Customer Service (Toll-Free) **1-888-454-2279**
💻 Visit **heinemannraintree.com** to browse our catalog and order online.

Editorial: Rebecca Rissman
Design: Kimberly R. Miracle and Joanna Hinton-Malivoire
Photo Research: Tracy Cummins and Tracey Engel
Production: Duncan Gilbert

Originated by Dot
Printed and bound by South China Printing Company
The paper used to print this book comes from sustainable resources.

ISBN-13: 978-1-4329-1589-6 (hc)
ISBN-10: 1-4329-1589-4 (hc)
ISBN-13: 978-1-4329-1599-5 (pb)
ISBN-10: 1-4329-1599-1 (pb)

12 11 10 09 08
10 9 8 7 6 5 4 3 2 1

**Library of Congress
Cataloging-in-Publication Data**
Harris, Nancy, 1956-
 Yellow / Nancy Harris.
   p. cm. -- (Colors)
Includes bibliographical references and index.
ISBN 978-1-4329-1589-6 (hc) -- ISBN 978-1-4329-1598-8 (pb) 1.
Yellow--Juvenile literature. 2. Color--Juvenile literature. I. Title.
  QC495.5.H379 2008
  535.6--dc22
                                      2008005607

Acknowledgments
The author and publisher are grateful to the following for permission to reproduce copyright material: ©Alamy **pp. 5** Bottom Right, **20, 22d, 23b** (Egmont Strigl); ©dreamstime.com **pp. 14, 23a** (Basslinegfx); ©Getty Images **pp. 11** (Royalty Free), **16** (GK Hart/Vikki Hart); ©istockphoto **pp. 4** Top Left (Willi Schmitz), **4** Top Right (Gasparetz Attila), **5** Bottom Left (Steve Dibblee), **5** Bottom Middle (Moritz von Hacht), **5** Top Right (Viktor Neimanis), **9** (robh), **13** (Annmarie Collette), **15** (Gez Browning), **21** (Reuben Schulz); ©Shutterstock **pp. 4** Bottom Left (Elen), **4** Bottom Middle (LouLouPhotos), **4** Bottom Right, **12, 22b** (Ariusz Nawrocki), **5** Top Left (Morozova Tatyana), **5** Top Middle, **6** (Konstantin Sutyagin), **7** (Anette Linnea Rasmussen), **10, 22a** (Gnuskin Petr), **17** (emin kuliyev), **18, 22c** (mdd), **19** (aaaah); ©SuperStock **pp. 4** Top Middle (Photographers Choice RF), **8** (Digital Vision Ltd.).

Cover photograph reproduced with permission of ©Getty Images/ Minden Pictures/Konrad Wothe.

Back cover photograph reproduced with permission of ©istockphoto/ Jim Jurica.

The publishers would like to thank Nancy Harris for her assistance in the preparation of this book.

Every effort has been made to contact copyright holders of any material reproduced in this book. Any omissions will be rectified in subsequent printings if notice is given to the publisher.

Disclaimer
All the Internet addresses (URLs) given in this book were valid at the time of going to press. However, due to the dynamic nature of the Internet, some addresses may have changed, or sites may have changed or ceased to exist since publication. While the author and publisher regret any inconvenience this may cause readers, no responsibility for any such changes can be accepted by either the author or the publisher.

Contents

Yellow

Are all plants yellow?

Are all animals yellow?

Are all rocks yellow?

Are all soils yellow?

Plants

Some leaves are yellow.

Some leaves are not yellow.

Some stems are yellow.

Some stems are not yellow.

Some flowers are yellow.

Some flowers are not yellow.

Animals

Some feathers are yellow.

Some feathers are not yellow.

Some scales are yellow.

Some scales are not yellow.

Some fur is yellow.

Some fur is not yellow.

Rocks

Some rocks are yellow.

Some rocks are not yellow.

Soil

Some soil is yellow.

Some soil is not yellow.

What Have You Learned?

Some plants are yellow.

Some animals are yellow.

Some rocks are yellow.

Some soils are yellow.

Picture Glossary

 **scale** small plate that covers the body of some animals

 **soil** mix of small rocks and dead plants. Plants grow in soil.

Content Vocabulary for Teachers

body covering	outer layer, such as skin or scales, that protects an animal
color	depends on the light that an object reflects or absorbs

Index

Note to Parents and Teachers

Before reading:
Talk with children about colors. Explain that there are many different colors, and that each color has a name. Use a color wheel or other simple color chart to point to name each color. Then, ask children to make a list of the colors they can see. After they have completed their list, ask children to share their results.

After reading:
Explain to children that yellow is a primary color. It cannot be created by mixing other colors together. Then, explain that yellow can be mixed with other primary colors to create secondary colors. Show students that yellow and red make orange, while yellow and blue make green.